# FUTURE READY
# INTERNET RESEARCH
# SKILLS

LYRIC GREEN and ANN GRAHAM GAINES

Published in 2018 by Enslow Publishing, LLC
101 W. 23rd Street, Suite 240, New York, NY 10011

**Library of Congress Cataloging-in-Publication Data**

Names: Green, Lyric, author. | Gaines, Ann Graham, author.
Title: Future ready internet research skills / Lyric Green and Ann Graham Gaines.
Description: New York : Enslow Publishing, 2018. | Series: Future ready project skills | Includes bibliographical references and index. |
Audience: Grade 3 to 6.
Identifiers: LCCN 2017001294| ISBN 9780766086555 (library-bound) | ISBN 9780766087699 (pbk.) | ISBN 9780766087705 (6-pack)
Subjects: LCSH: Internet research--Juvenile literature.
Classification: LCC ZA4228 .G74 2018 | DDC 001.4/202854678--dc23
LC record available at https://lccn.loc.gov/2017001294

Printed in China

**To Our Readers:** We have done our best to make sure all websites in this book were active and appropriate when we went to press. However, the author and the publisher have no control over and assume no liability for the material available on those websites or on any websites they may link to. Any comments or suggestions can be sent by email to customerservice@enslow.com.

Portions of this book were originally published in the book *Ace It! Master Your Internet Research Project.*

# CONTENTS

# CHAPTER 1

# THE WORLD WIDE WEB

It is a wonderful time to be alive! Twenty years ago, when people wanted to find information, they had to read about it in books, magazines, newspapers, or encyclopedias. Today we have a way to learn about everything in an instant. That's the World Wide Web! The World Wide Web lets us find information from—you guessed it—all over the world. People talk about the World Wide Web all the time. But many of us don't know the difference between the internet and the Web. The internet is a huge collection of computers around the world. These computers are connected to each other. People use the internet in many ways—writing email, instant messaging, sharing files, using social media, and surfing the Web. In order to surf the Web, you need a computer that's connected to the internet. The Web is part of the Internet.

Even though you'll use your computer for research, you should keep a notebook handy for any notes you want to take.

# WHAT IS THE WEB, ANYWAY?

It is made up of an enormous group of files called websites. Today, there are hundreds of millions of websites. Anyone can create one. People—or groups of people— use them to share words, pictures, music, movies, and information. You can visit the World Wide Web on any device with internet access. Computers can connect to the internet in different ways. Wi-Fi is the most common type of internet connection. Using Wi-Fi, computers, smartphones, and tablets can connect to the World Wide Web.

Besides internet access, you will also need a Web browser. This software makes it possible to view websites on your screen, once you have connected to the internet. Some popular Web browsers are Internet Explorer, Google Chrome, Firefox, and Safari. Many people use the Web for many different reasons. Kids use the Web to send email messages, to play games, or to create websites. They also use the Web to do research. Doing research means hunting for information.

Through the internet you can have a world of information at your fingertips!

# BEING SAFE ONLINE

Although the World Wide Web is a fun place to find new information, play games, and chat with friends, it can also be dangerous. Many websites are just for grownups. If you find

It's easy to access the Internet anywhere. Just connect from your device, and you're on your way!

one of these, close the window right away! Websites sometimes ask users to become a member of a group. If that happens, get help from an adult you trust. Also, never type your personal information into a website without getting permission from an adult. Personal information includes your name, age, address, phone number, email address, photo, or the name of your school. Never agree to get together with someone you met online. If someone you're chatting with online asks to meet in person, tell a parent or guardian immediately. People you meet on the Web might not be who they say they are. It is important always to think before you click.

Today, we can get on the web anywhere. Using a computer or tablet, we can surf the Web at home, in our classrooms, the library, even restaurants, airports, trains or airplanes!

## WHAT'S ON THE WEB?

The Web can be a powerful research tool. It can help you learn about animal shelters in your area, write an essay, enter a contest, work toward a goal, or keep track of your favorite musician. At school, your class might use computers to complete a Web quest. During a Web quest, students go online to hunt for information. It's like an online treasure hunt!

Using the Web can be fun and easy. It gives you information as fast as the click of a mouse. Be careful, though—the Web is not always the right source for your research. Not all resources on the web are reliable. And sometimes, believe it or not, you can often get information easier and quicker, by looking in the right book. If you need simple information—such as basic facts about tornadoes— you can save time by going to a book. It could be a reference book, like an encyclopedia. Or it could be a nonfiction book like this one.

Other times, it's a better idea to look on the Web first. Why? One reason is that the Web has a whole lot of information. There are millions and millions of websites, and they're created all over the world. Many experts create websites in order to share their knowledge with the world.

Another reason to use the Web is that it can give you brand new information. It is constantly growing. Every day, new Web pages go up. People often update their Web pages by adding current information. It's up to you to check the facts—but you'll never find a bigger collection of them! The Web can also be a starting point for more information. Let's say you are writing an essay about the history of your town. You can start by looking up your local records department or newspaper. From there, you should be able to find lots of other websites or places to look for more information.

A third reason to use the Web is that it has **multimedia** technology. *Multi* means "many." The word *media* means "a way to communicate information." So, multimedia technology is technology that uses lots of ways to communicate information. Websites can combine words with pictures, sounds, animation, and videos.

Researching on the Internet can be done anywhere, any time. Ask an adult to use a computer and have him or her help you with your Internet search.

Let's say you're interested in fennec foxes, for example. On the Web, you could read about fennec foxes. Then you could look at photos of them, watch a video of them in the wild, and hear the sounds they make—all on one site!

# CHAPTER 2

# ENDLESS INFORMATION

**A**ll websites have one thing in common: Every site is assigned its own **universal resource locator (URL)**. A URL is an address. If you know a website's URL, you can always find it. Just type the URL into the address line in a Web browser. Press the ENTER or RETURN button, and your browser will take you straight to that site.

## NAVIGATING THE WEB

There are many different kinds of websites. When you are doing research, you need to find informational websites. They give facts about one or more topics. Good informational websites are created by libraries, museums, schools, colleges, universities, government agencies, and other organizations. Later in this book, you'll learn how to look at a website's address to

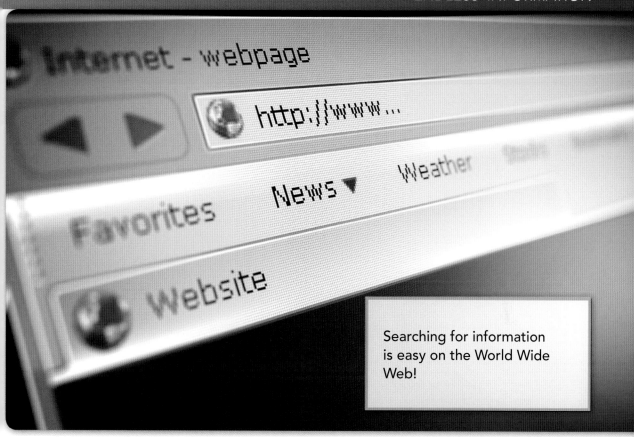

Searching for information is easy on the World Wide Web!

find out what kind of site it is. News sites are also helpful for researchers. These sites are created by newspapers, magazines, and television news stations. Some news sites include **blogs**. A blog is an online diary, journal, or source of news about a certain topic. Some journalists write blogs about their exciting experiences in the world. At the library, you can find special databases with collections of news articles from years ago.

What if you want learn about the history of your favorite cereal? Business sites give you information about a company's product—whether it's a movie, a CD, or a type of granola. Some business sites are especially entertaining for kids. Just beware: Businesses also use their websites to advertise their products to kids like you.

Personal websites are sites that individual people create. Be careful if you use a personal website. After all, anyone can put up a website. These sites are only helpful if the author knows a lot about a subject. If you're looking for reliable information, it needs to come from an expert. That's someone who has studied a subject for a long time. Later in this book, we'll discuss how to find out who created a website. Websites are made up of Web pages. These are a lot like the pages of a book. A website starts with a home page.

Just like you start your day at home, the home page is where you start your time on a website. Some home pages have a special feature called a **site map**. It shows you how the site is organized. Other home pages have a list of terms or

## ASK AN EXPERT!

One great thing about the internet is that it is much easier to contact experts. Many websites give you a chance to send a question to an expert. The National Park Service has a special page where you can write to a historian and ask a question about national parks or American history. Many colleges and research facilities allow you to do this, too. If you find the right site, you can even write to an expert from another country!

There are countless websites on the Internet. Whether you want to learn about your favorite TV show, play a game, or watch videos, you can find it on the Internet!

bullets on the side or along the top. The items on this list are called **hyperlinks**, or links for short. A link may be a word, a group of words, or a picture. Sometimes there are links in the middle of a paragraph, too. They are usually underlined or in a different color. When you see a link, move your cursor over it with the mouse. Your cursor will probably turn into a hand.

## TAKING NOTE

It is important to keep track of the information you find on the Web. Here are some helpful things to keep in mind:

Website name
Website address
Main links on the home page
Special features (images? videos?)
Date of creation

Then click on the link and it will take you to another page. This new Web page might be part of the same website, or it could belong to a different site. Don't worry about getting lost. Web browsers have a special BACK button. It lets you return to the page you were on before. Most Web pages have a title at the top. You'll also see some text at the bottom that says who created the website. Often you will see a date there. This tells you when the site was created or updated. Knowing a website's creator helps you decide whether you can trust the information. And knowing when it was last updated will help you determine if the information is up-to-date.

Before you start to do Web research, explore a few websites. This will help you understand how they're organized. Here are some suggestions for places to visit. The Library of

It's likely you'll learn all about Internet research very quickly and adults will soon come to you for help. Until then, ask an adult if you get stuck.

Congress American Memory site has many interesting historical papers, photographs, and artifacts to look at. The National Aquarium's site has information about visiting the aquarium and tells you about the many sea creatures that live there. Author Beverly Cleary's website has lots of information about her very funny books. FunBrain is a site with a lot of games to play.

# CHAPTER 3

# SEARCH ENGINES

Using the Web can be overwhelming. It takes some skill to find the information you want. There are lots of people who can help you learn to do research on the Web. Librarians are experts at searching for information. They know what you'll be able to find on the Web, and how to find it. Your teachers and family members can help, too. One good place to start your Web research is a search engine. A search engine is a website that helps you find information about the topic you choose. Some of the best search engines are Google.com and Yahoo.com.

The key to good Web research is knowing what you want to find out. First, think about your topic. Brainstorm a list of questions you'd like to answer. Once you've got a topic, you're ready to choose **keywords** for your Web research. Keywords are words that work like a key. They open up the door that leads you to the information you need.

Your librarian can help you with Internet research. Librarians are experts at finding information and may know sites to explore that you don't.

Sometimes your keywords will be obvious. Maybe you're looking for information about aardvarks. *Aardvark* will be your main keyword. Other times, your search is more complicated. Perhaps you want to learn about hockey in the United States. The keyword *hockey* is too broad. If you use it, you'll get too many websites that have to do with hockey from all over the world. Some won't even be in English! But if you use the keywords *hockey* and *USA*, the sites you get will match your topic.

## SEARCHING WITH A SEARCH ENGINE

How do search engines find you the information you need? They send out "spiders"! These are tools that make lists of words from websites. The search engine figures out which sites include each word most often. When you do a search, the search engine comes up with websites that use your keywords in many places. This is your results list.

Keywords can be too broad, but they can also be too narrow. If you want to know all about rodents, the keyword *hamster* won't give you enough information. There are lots of different rodents—not just hamsters.

Once you have a list of keywords, you're ready to start your Web search. Search engines are easy to use. Begin by typing the search engine's URL into your Web browser. Then look for a big blank box on the page. This box is often marked SEARCH. Type your keywords in the box and press ENTER. (If

# OUTER SPACE AND CYBERSPACE

Because the World Wide Web is constantly being updated, it can be a great place to learn about the latest scientific break-throughs. Maybe you're really in-terested in outer space. Science websites can offer more than a book can. You will find animation, videos, and lots of photos. Sites might also include games and activities that make learning fun. Some great plac-es to learn about space are NASA's site, or the Hayden Planetarium's site, where Neil deGrasse Tyson works. The information on these sites is updated daily and is reliable.

you're looking for an exact phrase, put it in quotation marks, like this: "violin strings.") In just a few seconds, the computer will show you a list of websites. For each site, you'll see a name and a short description. Scroll down to see more of the list. It might go on for several pages. Read some of the website descriptions. Do you think they will be helpful? Click on some of the links and visit the sites. If you don't see the information you want, do your search again. First, check to see if you spelled your keywords correctly. If that's not the problem, add another keyword—or change your keywords completely.

## KEYWORDS

Let's say you need to write a report about endangered honey bees. Using the right keywords can be very helpful. You might want to use words like honey, bees, or endangered animals. Be as precise as possible. It would be better to look for information on the honey bee in particular. If you use this phrase alone, you'll come up with sites that have too much information. If you use both *endangered species* and *honey bees*, you'll find a lot more information about when honey bees became endangered. Can you be even more specific? What do you think might harm the honey bee? Perhaps you wonder if they're in danger from pollution. Pollution would make an excellent keyword together with the others you already have.

You can use multiple keywords in one search. This way, you'll come up with information not just about the honey bee,

Grumpy Cat is an Internet celebrity.

but also why it's endangered.

## PHOTOS, VIDEOS, MUSIC—AND MORE

Another great thing about the Web is that you can find different forms of information. On websites you can find more than just written descriptions (text). You'll also see images— photographs, paintings, illustrations, diagrams, charts, maps, GIFs, and memes. Many sites include sound, video, and animation.

Let's talk about images first. Why might you want to find an image? Maybe you are trying to understand the difference between a red panda and a giant panda. Boy, would a photo help! An image would also be great to include in your research presentation. (If you take an image from a website, you have to get permission. More on that later.)

You can find images with a search engine. Many search engines let you search for only images. Google has a special images search page. You get there from the home page by using the IMAGES link. Type in your keywords—for example, *red panda*. Hit ENTER or click the SEARCH button. On the results page you will see **thumbnails**. These are photos so small that dozens fit on a single page. Click on a thumbnail you would like to use. Have an adult help you save, email, or print it. Many museums, magazines, and organizations like the Library of Congress, have image galleries on their websites.

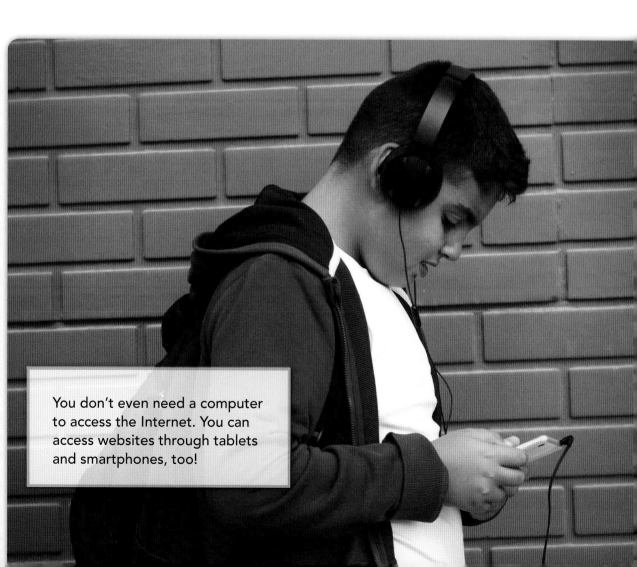

You don't even need a computer to access the Internet. You can access websites through tablets and smartphones, too!

These galleries work like smaller versions of a search engine.

The Web is a great place to search for videos. Maybe you've heard about an amazing ice-skating routine at the Olympics. Or perhaps you want to watch Martin Luther King, Jr. give his famous speech in front of the Lincoln memorial in 1963. There are two ways to find videos. You could use your search engine's special video search page. Or you can add the word *video* to your keyword search. You can even watch music videos, clips from television shows, and movie trailers online.

You can also look for music online. Look for a record company website and listen to samples. Then ask your parents if you can buy songs at an online music store like iTunes. If you like a specific band or singer, use a search engine to see if they have an official website and songs to download. You can also find speeches, podcasts, and other audio files on the Web.

It is possible to download pictures, music, and videos from the Web onto your computer. Remember, though, that it's not always safe to do so. Some file-sharing websites are illegal. Always ask permission from a trusted adult before downloading.

## UNDERSTANDING COPYRIGHT

When an author writes a book, she is granted a copyright. That means she is the legal owner of what she has written. If other people want to use her words, they have to get her permission. The same is true for art and music. That's why it's

If you're listening to music or watching videos in the library, be sure to use headphones so you don't disturb anyone.

wrong for individuals to put copies of songs onto file-sharing sites. Certain websites, like the Library of Congress and NASA will state if an image or quote is "fair use." This means that you have permission to use it. If you see the copyright symbol © , you will need to seek permission to use it.

# CHAPTER 4

# IS IT A GOOD OR BAD SITE?

Some websites are better than others. Carefully explore each site to see if you can trust the facts it gives you. The good news is: As you do Web research, you'll find lots of websites. Now the bad news: They're not all going to be helpful. You can run into all kinds of problems when you're doing research on the Web. Some sites won't be useful. They won't have the information you need. Worse yet, they might not be telling you all the facts or the truth!

You need to **evaluate** websites to determine if they are good for your project. That means you decide whether they are valuable and reliable. What does that mean? Why wouldn't a website be reliable? Remember, anyone in the world can create a website. Some people put wrong information on the Web on purpose, perhaps as a joke, or perhaps to mislead them. Sometimes a site is not reliable because the author

There are a lot of sites on the World Wide Web. Make sure you're using a site that is appropriate for someone your age.

does not understand the topic. Ask yourself these questions: Does it give the name of the person or organization who made the site? Does it say when the website was created? Was the site created by a school or a museum? If you can answer yes to all these questions, it's probably a good site.

If your parent, teacher, or librarian recommends a certain site, it's probably reliable. If you find a site on your own, you can ask an adult if it's a good one.

## CHECKING THE FACTS

Whatever sites you use, be sure and check the facts. In most cases, you should find more than one source about a certain topic. Even excellent sites can't provide all the facts on any one subject.

In order to make sure you're using a reliable website for information, look at its title to figure out its topic. Next, check to see who created it. The URL extension can give you a clue. The extension of a URL is the group of letters at the end, after the period (dot). If the extension is .edu, the site comes from a school. Another abbreviation is .com, for commercial. That means a business has put up the website. If you see .org, that stands for organization (like a museum or a church). Government websites end in .gov. American sites end in three letters. Sites created outside the United States end in two-letter abbreviations—.ca for Canada, .uk for the United Kingdom, .jp for Japan, and so on. Many websites are often translated into other languages. Google can even help you translate a website.

http://www.odnoklassniki.ru/

ОК одноклассники

The World Wide Web is named correctly: It is all over the world, in nearly every language!

It's best if you figure out exactly who created a site. This isn't always going to be possible, but you should try. Scroll down to the bottom of a Web page. There you might see the name of an author or an organization. You also might find copyright information, or even a link to an "About Us" page.

Also try to find out when the page was created. That information is not always available. But it's important if you need current information—for example, if you're trying to find out about the newest hit from your favorite singer or the latest information on weather. Other times, the date won't really matter. Just remember, though, that old websites might not have accurate information.

## MAKING YOUR OWN WEB PAGE

Have you ever thought about creating your own web page? Many very cool sites have been created by kids. Young authors use their sites to share information about their hobbies and interests. If you're interested in creating a web page, you'll first need to get permission from an adult at school or at home. An adult can help you make a website safely. After you have permission, decide what to put on your site. Write some text. Collect pictures (don't forget to get permission to use them, if they're not yours). Then go to the library to check out a book, or look for a website that explains how to create a web page.

## EVALUATING A WEBSITE

Web research can be a lot of fun, but it can also be frustrating. If you are not careful, you can lose track of some great information. Imagine that you're on one perfect Web page. It has the list of fascinating facts that you need for your school report. Then you follow a link to another Web page—and then another and another. Now you're lost! You can't get back to those fascinating facts.

# DOUBLE CHECKING CHECKLIST

- What is the address of the website? (The address usually starts with http://www.)
- Is the spelling correct?
- Are the author's name and e-mail address on the page? (This could be a person or an organization.)
- Are the links easy to find?
- Are the words easy to read?
- Is there a date that tells you when the page was made?
- Do the photographs look real and professional?
- Do the photographs on the site help you learn about the topic?
- Does the site tell you who took the photographs?
- Does the title tell you what the site is about?
- Does the site answer some of your research questions?
- Does the author of the page say things that you know are wrong?
- Does the author include a bibliography (a list of the sources he or she used to make the website)?

How can you keep this from happening? There are two ways you can look back at the websites you've visited. If you haven't quit your Web browser yet, you can use the BACK button. Now, let's say you already quit your Web browser, but you're still using the same computer. Open the browser back up. Click on the HISTORY button to see a list of every site you've been to recently. This will show you the name of each site and when you visited it.

## SAVING YOUR FAVORITE SITES

Many people use the same computer or device for all of their Web browsing needs. Your family might own one. Or you might have a computer you often use at your school, a library, or a youth center. If that's the case, you can create bookmarks or favorites using the Web browser. That means you'll add the website's title to a list. In the ADD TO FAVORITES or BOOK-MARK dialog box, you can see what name the site will be saved under or you can change that if you'd like.

Whenever you open the Web browser, you can go to your list of bookmarks or favorites. Select the title of the website you like, and the browser will take you right there. You can print out the information on a Web page if you want to use it later. Before you do so, use the PRINT PREVIEW command (under the File menu) to see what you'll actually be printing out. Printing is an excellent idea if you want to look at an entire Web page later. On the other hand, you could waste a lot of paper.

Take notes while you research. It will not only help you stay organized, but it will help you remember the information you find!

Only print what you really need. You don't want to waste paper. You can also take notes from websites in your own notebook. Make sure to record the URL, the name of the site, the date it was created, and the date you used it. You may want to write down the author of an article or the site, too. Also take notes on the interesting information you have found. You could make your notes in a word processing program, in a notebook, or on note cards.

# CHAPTER 5

# USING WHAT YOU FIND

There is one very important thing to remember while taking notes. Never write information word for word unless you put it in quotation marks. If you use someone else's words without quotation marks, you are **plagiarizing**. Plagiarizing is not just bad research, it is also illegal.

When taking notes, it is important to only write down the most important pieces of information. Say you're doing a report on Ridley sea turtles. As you read information on websites, you may want to only note the size of the turtle, where it lives, what it eats, and what it looks like. If you're doing a report on the author E. B. White, you may want to note when he lives, where he lives, notes about his family and education, and his most famous books.

You will do a lot more Web research throughout your life. At first, you might feel like you don't know what to do. Don't

You may have to present your research to your classmates or teacher. Your presentation will be better if you've done the right kind of research!

worry! Over time you will gain skill. Your Web research will get better and better. You'll also find more and more ways to use this skill. Web research can help you write great stories and reports, put together interesting presentations, and find out more about your hobbies and interests. Enjoy!

## PLAGIARISM—HOW TO AVOID IT

What is plagiarism? That's when you use someone's else's work or words and do not give them the credit they deserve. This can happen if you're not very careful when you take notes. Never copy exact sentences from a source—unless you see something that you want to quote. If you do quote someone else's words, use quotation marks around the words. Write the name of the person who said them. For example, write: *Veterinarian Dr. Nora Henry says, "Always make sure your pet is up to date with their shots."* Finally, make sure to include the source of the quote in your bibliography.

Plagiarism is a serious problem. If your teacher thinks you have plagiarized without understanding why it is wrong, she might let you redo your work. But many teachers will give your paper a very low grade or a zero.

Always take note of the site's name, author and date created (if you can find it), the URL, and the date when you visited the site.

Don't be intimidated by a research project. They can be fun. And you never know what you'll discover while researching!

Sometimes, you may have to do a group research project. This will allow everyone to gather information and compile it for a great project!

# A WORLD OF WEBSITES

There are millions upon millions of websites on the internet. Imagine all those images, videos, and information at your fingertips! It is best to be cautious when searching the Web, but remember that it can be fun, too! Soon, you'll be an expert at finding exactly what you need.

# GLOSSARY

**bibliography**  A list of sources used in a paper or other research project.

**database**  A large collection of information.

**evaluate**  To make a decision about how valuable or correct something is.

**extension**  A dot (period) plus the last two or three letters at the end of a URL—i.e., .gov, .edu, .com.

**home page**  The first page you see when you enter the main URL for a website.

**hyperlinks**  Words or images on a website that lead to a new location, such as another website, when you click on them.

**internet**  A worldwide system of networked, or linked, computers.

**keywords**  Words or phrases that you use to begin a search on the Web.

**multimedia**  Using more than one way to display information at a time for example, mixing words with photographs, music, and video.

**network**  A group of objects that are linked together.

**plagiarizing**  Taking someone else's work and presenting it as your own.

**reference book**  A book that contains facts about general topics or words, like a dictionary or an encyclopedia.

**research**  A search for information about a certain topic.

**samples**  Small parts of songs or other sound files.

**scroll**  To move up and down on a computer screen.

**search engine**  A website that finds pages with information about a certain topic, based on a keyword search.

**source**  Material that provides information, such as a book, magazine, song, website, piece of art, or interview with a person.

**surfing**  Exploring the World Wide Web by going from one site to another.

**thumbnails**  Photographs that are about the size of a grownup's thumbnail.

**URL**  A website address.

**Web browser**  A computer program that allows users to surf the internet, such as Google Chrome or Firefox.

**website**  A collection of Web pages that is reached through an introductory or home page.

**World Wide Web**  A network of documents (also known as sites) that are available on the internet.

# FURTHER READING

## BOOKS

Greenberg, Michael. *Painless Study Techniques*. Hauppauge, NY: Barron's Educational Publishing, 2016.

Jakubiak, David J. *A Smart Kid's Guide to Doing Internet Research*. New York, NY: Powerkids Press, 2009.

Marji Majed. *Learn Program with Scratch: A Visual Introduction to Programming with Games, Art, Science, and Math*. San Francisco, CA: No Starch Press, 2014.

McManus, Sean. *How to Code in 10 Easy Lessons: Learn How to Design and Code Your Very Own Computer Game*. Minneapolis, MN: Walter Foster, Jr. (Lerner Press), 2015.

Randolph, Ryan. *New Research Techniques: Getting the Most Out of Search Engine Tools*. New York, NY: Rosen Publishing, 2011.

# WEBSITES

**American Library Association**

http://gws.ala.org

A list of recommended sites for kids on many topics.

**Discovery Kids**

http://discoverykids.com

Games, videos, and information about everything from animals to space.

**Kids.gov**

https://kids.usa.gov

A government-run website that covers many topics including science, history, art, music, and more!

**PBS**

http://pbskids.org

Shows, videos, games, and information about many subjects!

# INDEX